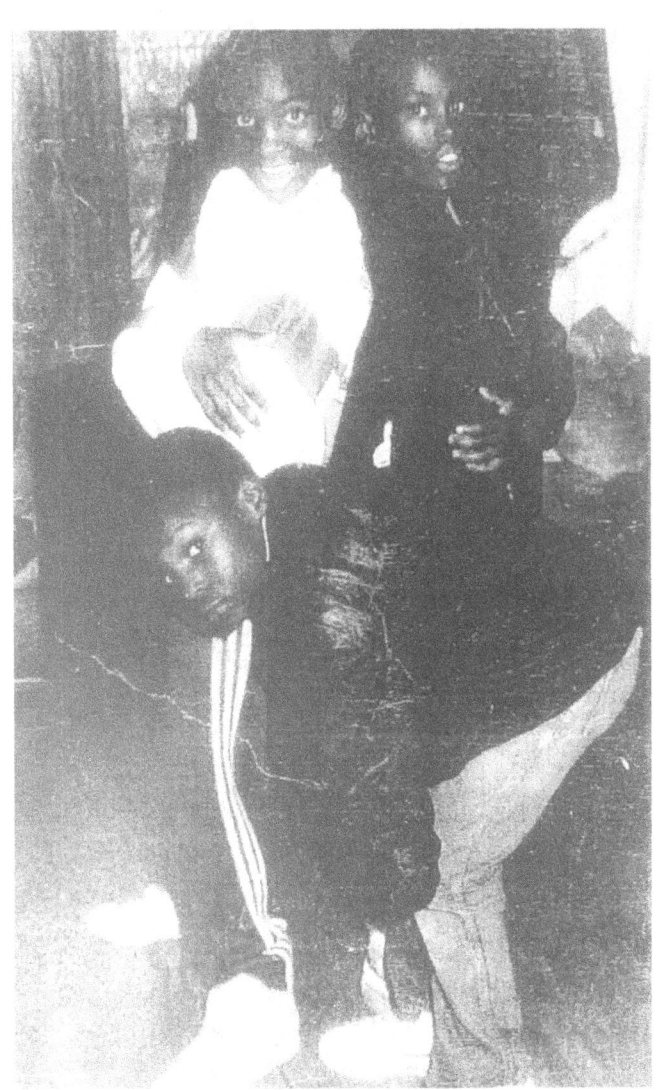

The Writings of Bobby Bostic

TABLE OF CONTENTS

Make History While You Make Yourself 3
The Faith Behind the Man 6
Leadership   Part 1 8
Bad Kids: Should We Lock Them Up and Throw Away the Key 12
Live From the School to Prison Pipeline 19
Reading Makes You Free 22
Language is Deeper than Words 25
Crime Control in the Age of Mass Incarceration . 29
Through the Darkness Find the Light Within You 35
Unsung Heroes 37
Sometimes You Have to Climb a Mountain to Get There 39
Never Judge a Book by Its Cover 41
A Mother's Burden   9-18-2020 44
A GARDEN in the Ghetto 46
When Adults can be Kids Again (While Having Fun) 7-26-2021   50
A Piece of Peace 7-26-2021 52
Internal Value v. External Value 54
The Making of a Classic 57
The Responsibility of Being a Parent 65

All My Life	68
The Art of GARDENING	70
You will Become Someone's Mother One Day	73
Vision: Coming into Focus	75
Forged from Pain (Ode to Aretha Franklin) 2-12-2021	77
Nothing Like	79
Domestic Household Politics 11-15	80
The Water of Woman's Tears 11-13-21	82
What you Go Through Helps You Get Through 1-14-21	84
Dreams Die if We Let Them Sleep	86
Vision: Coming Into Focus 12-9-2021	88
Through the Darkness Find the Light Within You 9-18-2020	91

Make History While You Make Yourself

We should always have our eyes pointed toward history. It is the yardstick by which we should measure the progress of the world as well as our own lives. There is good history and there is bad history. History repeats itself, the question for you to answer is: which side of history would you like to be on. We all have goals for which we are striving to achieve. What this means is that we have not reached fulfillment in our lives. IN order to reach our plateau there are conditions and things about our lives that we need to change. While doing this you must expand your range. YOU must try to do something that has never been done before. Remember that with each milestone that you reach, you are knocking on history's door.

It doesn't require becoming a historic figure in order to make history. Just remind yourself that you are history in the making. With this in mind, envision yourself doing something paramount. Each one of us has something unique to offer to the world that only you as an individual can give. What is your gift or particular skill set? Have you even begun to tap that inner resource to develop your particular gift so that you can give that to the world? If the answer to this question is no, then you should heed this call to make history while remaking yourself.

History is being made everyday. We must begin to ask ourselves where do we fit into this picture? Time is passing by each day. This is why you must create opportunities for yourself. Even if you work hard, then you can work even harder. It takes extra energy and motivation to excel to your fullest potential. DO not set your sights on being average, you must strive for greatness. Symbolically climb mountains that only you can reach the peak. Capitalize off of that character trait that makes you unique. There is something that only you can do in this life. That is your life purpose that you were born for. You must not abandon that.

Even as you remake yourself don't forget the picture that is bigger. As you go through this transformation it will be more difficult than anything you've ever encountered before. It requires you to challenge yourself in ways that will stretch you beyond your known limits. This puts you to the test of knowing for certain that there is no limit to what you can accomplish. With this realization you go into the world with the mentality that there is nothing you can't do. You will push yourself on to do more than you ever thought you could do. This re-invention of yourself is a historic point in your own individual life. As you do this, you will begin to look outside of your own self and see the change that you could effect in the larger world. In fact you will soon see the many changes that are needed in this world. You will see empty gaps in contemporary history where your own efforts to change the world could fit into.

This will require way more energy and effort than you had to put into remaking yourself. Now you will have to triple your efforts and work ethic. You must fly to new heights as you reach your zenith. Go to the distance as if your life depended on it. Broaden the scope beyond yourself because history has to be made. YOU don't have to become a politician, famous artist, or athlete to make history. It's everyday people who live ordinary civilian lives that make their own history by coming out of their shell and doing historic things in seemingly miraculous ways. So do you want to make history? Do you want to achieve greatness in your life? If so you must start by remaking yourself. I have laid out an embryo & the blueprint on how you as an individual can make your own history in this world. YOU must give life to this embryo by first changing those things about yourself that get in your own way of you reaching your potential in life. You have to overcome those personal obstacles that prevent you from totally believing in your ability to achieve greatness. Once you remake and redo those things about yourself then you can make history in the process from a local scale to a global scale. You were born into this world for a reason. This world needs what only you as an individual can do for it. That is your life purpose. As you come into this knowledge through wisdom and experience your life journey will then allow you to make history while remaking yourself

The Faith Behind the Man

To the uninitiated, it seems amazing how he turns defeat into victory
But for those who in tune with Go,1 his success is not a mystery
It is all done by God's Grace
While playing the cards he was dealt this was his ace

When all odds were against him something kept pushing on inside
Deep within his soul is where his faith reside
It carried him through the storm when he should've been broken
He tuned out the worldly noise and listened when a Higher Power had spoken

People only look! to his exterior while not paying attention to his faith
Not understanding how he goes these battles coming out without a scathe
Those without faith who are around him come out all bruised and battered
With no strong anchor their inner harbors are tattered

When times got hard he had a plan to conceive
He relied on God's power while others didn't believe
In his struggles is a definite lesson for me as well as you

Even though it was hard he somehow made it
look easy
The pace that he ran through life's troubles would
make the unfaithful tired and wheezy
From the outside looking in he seemed like the
least likely to have the

Leadership Part 1

A leader is by definition a person who works though other people to achieve a goal or a vision. A president sets a vision or direction for the nation, then commissions his staff and his cabinet to achieve that vision, and works with Congress to enact that vision. A corporate CEO articulates a vision for the company, works through the management team to implement that vision, and motivates the workforce to fulfill that vision at every level.

Every leader stands on the shoulders of giants. The leader is greater than the follower. A leader cannot accomplish all of his goals without the help of gifted followers. A true leader sacrifices his or her followers. Leaders are people of vision. A leader sees a future that no one else can see and then takes his followers there. There, his followers help turn his action and turn his vision into a reality.

Sometimes doing the right thing doesn't seem ltke the correct thing to do. Martin Luther King, Jr. once said that a true leader Is not a seeker of consensus, but a molder of consensus. In other words, a leader is a trailblazer and has to go against the grain to chart a trajectory in life. Us being here today is going against the prison grain of standing around the yard talking and playing sports.

We had to have a vision or wanted something more out of life that we flgured we could learn in this class today. We are thinking outside of the box. We are demonstrating that first essential character of leadership. Remember that a leader is a servant of the people. Therefore he must be willing to share his time, attention, and experience. He can do this by being someone's mentor. Each one of us should mentor someone who is less experienced than we are. We should also seek the mentorship of people who are more experienced than we are In various fields of life. 70 percent of all authentic leaders throughout history said that a mentor is partially responsible for their success.

    There are steps that each leader must take before he gets to where he is trying to go. He can't skip over the steps, he must go through the process. If we try to take more steps than one then we will trip over the other steps that we need to take. Once we fall off of those steps then we set ourselves back. There are no shortcuts to the process of success. This is what we as leaders must show our followers. And any smart leader does not try to take all of the credit. The team will give him his proper recognition for his leadership

    Sometimes a leader must stand alone, and even his supporters will oppose his plan. This is why being a leader can get lonely. So many decisions rest on your shoulders and whatever decision that you make affects the fate of many people. So it isn't easy being a leader, it is a role that comes with much responsibility.

    People often glamorize people in leadership roles, or envy people in those roles. But it takes much work and sacrifice to be a leader. It is more difficult than it looks from the outside looking in.

Leaders change the world, not their critics. As a leader you must be an innovator for change. There are many leaders in this very room. Some of you are natural leaders, the others must be molded and monitored to bring out their leadership capabilities. Some of you never thought of ourselves as leaders but there have been events in your life that forced you to take in a leadership role and you excelled in that role.

It has been wisely said that the purpose of leadership is to produce more leaders. We must turn today's followers into tomorrow's leaders. We want our followers to reach higher heights than we ever reached in life. That is the proper legacy of regal leadership. And with that sort of leadership and impact we can move our followers into action to change the world.

By a leader being prepared for his journey, he also prepares the way for those who follow him. So remember those steps. They must be climbed in order to reach the top. When you get there, a real leader will take you to even higher heights. His vision is always on higher horizons. Another characteristic of leaders is that they know how to forgive. You must learn to forgive people if you hope to work with them. In the business world sometimes you have to work with people that you do not like or agree with. How can we work with them if we are holding grudges against them? The best way to get over your animosity is to focus on the common ground that you and that person must stand on in order to reach your respective goals. It is not easy but must be done in order to ensure your success.

Leadership requires us to see what we have to do, then work hard to get it done. If we are to serve the people then we have to do that hard work that comes with that obligation. Everything that a leader achieves is through team achievements because a leader needs his team to achieve his goals. It is not the coach who wins the game. It is the team. It is not the CEO who earns the profit but it is the company that earns the profit. It is the soldiers who win those battles, not the general who directs them.

We know that this world needs strong honest leaders more than ever. We are disgusted with the political scandals and we especially need leaders in that arena. In the industry we see multiple scandals in banking and other areas. Quality leadership can turn all of these industries in the right direction. The purpose of today's seminar has been to teach the audience how to take the initial steps of becoming effective leaders. We hope you have learned something toward that goal today that will inspire you to become tomorrow's EFFECTIVE LEADER.

Bad Kids: Should We Lock Them Up and Throw Away the Key

Currently there are over 2,500 Juveniles (anyone who was under the age of 18 years old when they committed their crime) serving a sentence of life without parole for homicide in the United States. ("Rest of Their Lives") In addition to this there are three thousand more serving de facto life without parole.sentences (a sentence of many decades in prison beyond the juveniles life expectancy) for violent crimes that did not involve murder. (Graham v. Florida). Before I express my viewpoint on this issue I want to ask the readers a question. Do you feel that juveniles who commit heinous crimes should die in prison? Now before you answer that question, please give it considerable thought as you reflect on it. Do you have a family member who is a troubled teen who is involved in pretty crime or delinquent acts? If those acts turn violent, would you want him to spend the rest of their lives in prison?

However there are always two sides to an argument. What if you were the family member of a victim who was senselessly murdered by a juvenile defendant? Where would you stand on the issue then? Even if you feel that they should be harshly punished for what they did to your loved one; do you think that there is any hope that they could one day change? You are entitled to whatever answer you may choose to these questions, Before you firmly commit yourself to a stance on this issue I would like to express a few notions I have in this regard after briefly giving you the facts,

When we think of kids we don't often associate them as being criminals. Somehow in today's turbulent world that is changing. Crime does exist and some kids will gravitate towards it. The first Juvenile delinquent courts in this country were first established in the early 1900's'. In further decades, as Juvenile crime progressively rose; more and more kids were certified to stand trial as adults. Although they were still technically juveniles; the criminal justice system treated them as adults, Fast forward to the 1980's and 1990's when crime reached an all time high; particularly Juveniles' crime. In fact, criminologists carved out a special niche for this particular class of youth offenders, deeming them as the "super-predators", This resulted in a huge uplink of Juveniles being sentenced to life without parole sentences, de facto life without parole sentences and even the death penalty

Gangs entered into the picture and for the most insignificant of reasons, kids started killing other kids. Society became aware of its kids while at the same time becoming afraid of them. In response, they were given harsher sentences in the criminal justice system. Meanwhile in the rest of the world; countries moved away from sentencing Juveniles as adults while moving toward treatment for them. The death penalty, and Juvenile life without parole as well as de facto life without parole was done away with in the majority of developed countries. In fact, as of today, the United States is the lone country who sentences juveniles to life without parole. ("Sentencing Our Children to Die in Prison".)

Enter the United States Supreme Court. As the Highest Court in the land, it sets the legal precedent for this country as to what can or cannot be legally done per the United States Constitution. In 2005 the High Court entered this controversial debate by declaring it unconstitutional to sentence juveniles to the death ponalty. (Roper v. Simmons). The Court held: "Three general differences between juveniles under 18 and adults demonstrate that juvenile offenders cannot with reliability be classified among the worst offenders."' The Court cited scientific and sociological studies to uphold its position that (1) Juveniles has lessened culpability, therefore tlrey are less deserving of the most severe punishments. (2) As youth have a lack of maturity and underdeveloped sense responsibllity, they are more vulnerable to negative influences and outside pressures, including peer pressure. (3) The character traits of juveniles are not as well formed as that of an adult, making them much more llkely for rehabilitation.

After the Court's prohibition of the death penalty for juveniles, the harshest sentence that they could receive was life without parole. Not only for murder, but also for other crimes such as robbery, rape, armed burglary, vast drug conspiracy, etc. This led the United States Supreme Court to enter into the fray again in 2010. In the case *Graham v. Florida*, the Court held that the Eighth Amendment's Cruel and Unusual Punishment Clause prohibited the states from sentencing juveniles to life without parole for non-homicide crimes. (*Graham v. Florida*). Basing its ruling on much of the factors outlined in its Roper decision as well as updated scientific factors the Court said that states must at least give these children the chance to one day show that their childhood crimes does not define who they are; and therefore give them a chance to prove that they are eligible for release before their life ends.

Two years later, the Court made yet another stance on this issue in the case of *Miller v. Alabama*, ("*Miller v. Alabama*"). In that ruling that the court prohibited states from automatically giving Juveniles life without parole for homicide convictions without first considering mitigating factors. It left open the states to have the opportunity to give Juveniles life without parole in only the rare case where the courts found that a juvenile was incorrigible beyond repair. Four years later the Court again pushed reluctant states towards its reasoning by making its *Miller* ruling retroactive in the case of *Montgomery v. Louisiana*, ("*Montgomery v. Louisiana*"). It told state courts: "that before enforcing a Juvenile to life without parole, the sentencing judge must take into account how children are different, and how those differences counsel against sentencing them to a lifetime in prison", etc. The Court further said: "the opportunity for release will be afforded to those who demonstrate that children who commit even heinous crimes are capable of change."

Despite all of the above Court rulings we still have at least 2,500 juveniles serving life without parole as well as around 3,000 others serving de facto life without parole. Now that I have given you a very brief history dealing wlth this sentencing practice, we now arrive back where we began: should kids be sentenced to die in prison? Well it all depends on who you ask. The tough on crime proponents spew rhetoric such as, "do the crime, do the time" or "if they are old enough to kill, then they are bold enough to die in prison," etc. Rightfully alongside them are the actual victims of crimes and their family members who have an immediate stake at issue. Then there is society in general.

Kids do not think things through. Juveniles make very irrational decisions without taking into consideration the long term effects. Edven in the case where they kill; sometimes it takes months if not years for their maturity to set in to allow them to show sufficient empathy and experience meaningful remorse. Modern science proves everything that I am saying. ("Age Difference in Future Orientation and Delay"). Neurologicalogist Lawrence Steinberg wrote: "changes in impulse control and planning are mediated by a cognitive control network which matures more gradually and over a longer period of time, into early adulthood." (Steinberg).

Critics may claim that I am making excuses for those violent juveniles. I have merely stated proven scientific facts. To argue with my position is to argue against science; thereby forfeiting logic as well as reason. Yet I will not be dogmatic or one-sided in my stance on this issue. What if I were to put myself in the victim's shoes (or their family members)? How would I feel then? If I was strictly contained; I would still dislike the juvenile defendant who committed this terrible crime. Nevertheless I would always keep in mind that the person who committed this crime was a child. If they show remorse and redeeming qualities I would come around to the view that they are worthy of second chances one day.

Windicitive judges in many states have skirted around the Supreme Court's prohibition on life without parole sentences by instead trying juveniles whereby the judge gives them a de facto life without parole sentence. When a juvenile is sentenced to multiple decades in prison or even hundreds of years, there is no way in which they'll be able to live to see their parole date because it is set beyond their life expectancy. As Kelly Scavone vividly states in her law journal: "Although virtual life without parole sentences are not categorically barred for juvenile homicide offenders under Miller, lengthy sentences without parole eligibility create the exact result that the court was trying to avoid in Miller and Graham. Juveniles must be afforded individualized sentencing hearings that account for their mitigating factors of youth, and in the majority of cases, must be given an opportunity to reenter society before spending their entire lives behind bars." Therefore de facto life without parole is not a viable solution to the problem. Some states have adapted to a reasonable format by implementing laws whereby life sentenced juveniles can go see the parole board after serving 25 years of their sentence. This is a sufficient solution.

Furthermore, seeing the parole board does not automatically mean that they will be released. What it does is at least give them an opportunity. Henceforth, it will be up to that former juvenile to show that they have been rehabilitated and will be a productive member of society if they are released. Parole will serve as a slight czech and balance on their progress in the free world. What I propose is not a get out of jail free card. I hold that these juveniles must be held accountable. Once they have sufficiently shown remorse, paid their dues to society, and rehabilitated themselves; I say we should give them a second chance. It makes no sense to waste taxpayers' money by holding them in prison until they die. They deserve a second chance. Bad kids can become good adults. We shouldn't lock up our children and throw away the key.

Live From the School to Prison Pipeline

The school to prison pipeline is not just a theory. It is not something that social scientists conjured up. It is real life. I write these from my prison cell in the pipeline to let you know the truth of this experience. What is the school to prison pipeline? Is it as simple as it sounds? Are kids pushed from school through a pipeline straight to prison? Well I don't want to make it sound so cruel but it can happen that way. How does this happen? I don't want to place the blame on society or the government for the mistakes that young teenagers make by committing crimes that eventually land them in an adult prison.

The school-to-prison pipeline is a combination of factors. It starts in the communities where inadequate schools are built. Many of these schools are segregated. These schools are often underfunded, overcrowded, and deteriorating. ("The Impact of Racially Inclusive Schooling in Adult Incarcerated Rates Among U.S. Cohorts of African Americans and Whites Since 1930"). Such conditions heighten their chances of being incarcerated in adulthood. Many of the males in these communities are unemployed. Such strains on relationships lead to divorce. Therefore, single mothers are left to mentors. There are situational factors that can enter them into crime. The main factors include peers, thrills, excitement, experience, learning, and economic opportunity. ("Unstructured Socializing and Rates of Delinquency").

Their community cohesiveness became destabilized. All they see is media advertisements that link success to having the best material possessions. However they lack the means and resources to obtain these material possessions. Not wanting to be powerless these youth turn to crime to obtain these material possessions. When they start committing crimes, they often drop out of school. When they are caught for these crimes in their mid teens they get certified and these teenagers were in school or dropped out of school for a year or two prior to committing their crimes. They go straight from school to prison.

Troubled teenagers tend to seek out other troubled teenagers and this causes them to get into even more trouble when they get together for the inappropriate purpose of engaging in more troublesome antisocial behavior. ("Delinquent Peer Influence on Offending Versatility: Can Peers Promote Specialized Delinquency"). For teenage girls who engage in these behaviors it can lead to promiscuous activities which lead to them having kids .With their lack of parental skills they can end up raising troubled delinquents themselves, thereby perpetuating the cycle. ("Young Mothers, Delinquent Children: Assessing Mediating Factors Among American Youth").

Schools play a prominent part in the school to prison pipeline. Many high schools in poverty stricken ghettos have a high school completion rate of 40 percent. There have been around 1,800 of these schools documented in america. These schools make up half of all the high school dropouts in this country every year. Thus they have been labeled as dropout factories. ("Building a Grad Nation: Progress and Challenge in Ending the High School Dropout Epidemic"). Some of these kids suffer developmental abilities which were ignored or they were written off as lazy. Their low cognitive skills combined with the disdain they felt was shown to them caused them to be disinterested in school. When you combine this with kids who did not go back after suspension, expulsion, or pregnancy the "dropout effect" is significantly increased. ("Drug Use and Delinquency: Causes of Dropping Out of High School?") Exacerbating this problem is the unfair disciplinary infractions given to African American children versus their peers. Such unfair treatment causes these students to rebel. When they rebel and drop off of school it leads to them engaging in more delinquent activities which eventually leads to them committing crime. ("Does Dropping out of School Mean Dropping Into Delinquency"). When they are caught they end up in jail and eventually go to prison. ("Understanding the Antecedents of the School to Jail Link: The Relationship Between Race and School Discipline").

Reading Makes You Free

How can I explain the joy that I get from reading? Words can't explain it. Nevertheless, here in my speech today I will express in human language what reading means to me and how it has made me free even while inside of prison. Locked in a cell for twenty four hours a day when I was 16 years old I had no company except the books tha tI had in my cell. When I picked those books up I discovered a much larger world than the one I had always limited myself to on the streets in my city of St. Louis, Missouri. Reading allows me to go wherever I want to on the facts of the universe. Books take me to so many places. The books I have read opened up worlds to me that I didn't even know existed.

It is difficult to explain the feelings that you get from reading. Emotionally books make you feel whole. You can find your life's purpose between these pages. When you read you get feelings that can be likened to love. This is how deep and meaningful reading is. As you read the stories of someone else, you wonder how did the author know your own story so well although he was writing about someone else. How does that author know your thoughts as if he or she was already inside of your mind? When we read about history the author takes us back in time and we feel like we are right there on the scene reliving those events again. Reading is better than a movie. The page just takes you away. This is how we get lost in the words as we read. For me, life on the page is real because I feel what the author is talking about. Reading lives inside of your heart. I can feel it just as I am taking a breath now and have sight to see. This is what reading does for me. It does more than just pass time, it surpasses time. Reading has no limits and it is endless. If it were not for words and language, how can functions? This is why I promote reading the way that I do with extreme passion. Reading changes people's lives and causes them to excel to their highest heights. There is power in words. Reading helps us to see a clearer path, it inspires us to want to become better when we read about someone else accomplishing their goals. Reading is ecstasy. Reading gives us a natural high. It is intellectual intoxication. There are no side-effects. There is no coming down from this high. YOU just stay high, just turn the page and get even higher. This is why I love reading. What about you?

The mind is a wonderland. It allows you to go where you want to go despite our incarceration. Books take us to places that we have never been or seen. We read books from centuries ago and feel as if we are right there as it is going down.

The mind is like a machine that is always turning, always coming up with new ideas and creative means of ways of doing things. I love reading. I read some of everything. Books are my sanctuary. Reading is where I find peace and meaning. The more books that I read, the more that I find myself. It seems like the book that I read is the exact book that I needed to read at exactly the moment that Iread that particular book.

Books and reading can make us free. It was books that lifted me out of prison. My 240 year sentence is no longer my destiny. Books allow me to see beyond my time. Life is bigger than prison and books will teach you that. The authors seem to put words that you have wanted to express your entire life.

The right sources of reading can make any man free. It is like the old saying of an older person drinking from the fountain of youth. Reading revives and heals the soul.

Malcolm X said that when he was in prison, books opened up a new world to him. He said that from that moment on he read with every second of free time he had on his hand. This is because reading made him free. In fact, he said that he did so much reading that the months passed without him even thinking of the fact that he was in prison. He said that at that point in his life he was truly free, and had never been freer in his entire life.

At first, he read without a particular aim. Then he began to read selectively with a purpose. He said that he knew right there in prison that reading changed the course of his life forever. He also said that reading awoke in him a craving to be mentally alive. He said that if he could just spend the rest of his life reading books that he would do just that to satisfy his curiosity. This was a man that understood the importance of reading.

We also must come to understand the importance of reading and how it will affect the course of our lives from this moment on forward. Man, I was telling you that reading can make us free, free from ignorance, free from mediocrity, freedom from not having a purpose, freedom from slavery. Reading can surely make us free.

Language is Deeper than Words

We sometimes experience emotions of a spiritual nature that is difficult to verbalize and put into words. The ultimate aim of language usage is to express more deeply and directly the emotions that we feel. Look at how music speaks to us. Even the beat speaks to us. Each instrument has its own voice. This is why I say that language is deeper than words.

Language is the exterior design of our unconscious and nonverbal thought process. Animals have a special language that they express through their bodies and movements. Look at how the lion hunts on the safari. Look at the deer when it runs out of fear, etc.

According to many language experts all languages share certain features, which they call Universal Grammar. They also say that languages have what is known as recursion, which means putting phrases inside phrases: such as "the food you are eating smells good. Some indigenous people have a saying that says: "the things that go on in your head when you sleep." To us, this means to dream But to them, it means a new experience. For them dreaming is a real experience as real as the moments that they are awake. It is not fiction. It is real to them.

Experts in language have discovered from extensive research that language is defined by the culture in which people live. Through mirror neurons in the brain we can place ourselves in someone else's experience and imagine their experience. This is what we attempt to do through language when we tell stories.

Before language was invented in ancient times, our ancestors had to communicate with each other. They had to form groups to build shelter, hunt, and gather food. They did all this without using words. This is another reason why I say that language is deeper than words. Our ancestors developed this institution hundreds of thousands of years before the invention of language. This is the same intelligent experience we feel when we say "I can't put it into words."

Without words people's behavior can communicate to us. We can sense people's moods as they walk into a room without them even saying a single word. Much of what we see around us is nonverbal. We call it unspoken language. Again language is deeper than words. Then we have what we call body language, which is all the signals people reveal nonverbal. We have an interior monologue that allows us to pick up signals from people that register to us as feelings or sensations.

What we read nonverbally in body language sometimes tells us a lot about people's psychology. That goes back to the saying of "Actions speak louder than words." Don't just talk about it, but walk it. Our successful actions in life speaker louder than our words or simple plans of success. Mean what you say and say what you mean.

Sometimes people wear masks and disguise their intentions. If you can see beyond their masks then their language is deeper than words. Even the way that people dress sends you nonverbal clues about them. If people keep themselves organized and well groomed it sends you signals about them. However, first impressions can be tricky. People say that we should go off of their first impressions, but that is often not always true. People can present themselves one way today but tomorrow can act differently. This is true for each human being. Sometimes we may be in a bad mood or have something serious on our minds.

We have a public persona and we have a private persona. In public people wear a harder exterior to protect themselves. In private they are more relaxed. We must get a picture of someone's character over time. In our preconceived notions we often misunderstand people, especially quiet people. We fail to understand them, or see their deep depths because they don't talk that much.

To develop our intelligence we must start to think in terms of visual images. Language is a system designed for social communication. But sometimes, language can fail us. There are many concepts that have no particular world in the English language to describe them. Language can be too tight or constricted as compared to the multilayered intelligence that humans have. Therefore we must develop the ability to think beyond language. Images give us fluid ideas that we can later verbalize. Images are straightforward and clear while words are abstract. We cannot justify thinking in words. We must expand our thinking and fine tune our senses because language is deeper than words.

Crime Control in the Age of Mass Incarceration

Locking criminals up and throwing away the key will not solve the crime problem. Statistics show that although incarceration rates have increased, but crime continues to decrease, We do have a serious crime problem in this country that needs to be addressed. Crime presents a social harm that poses a threat to all elements of society. ("Deviant Behavior"). In this paper I point out the unfairness in which those in power address the crime epidemic. Street crimes are often heavily punished with stiff penalties. On the other hand white-collar crimes cause more social harm to society but they are often punished with minor penalties. ("Unravelling Bias in Arrest Decisions"). Such inequality in the criminal justice system is what leads to the current crisis of mass incarceration.

In order to solve crime we must address Its root causes. Poverty is at the root cause of most street economic crimes. ("The Culture Of Poverty"). It starts in childhood for those most affected by this. ("Effects of Poverty on Children') ,these entire communities become "hollowed out". ("Expanding Coupled Shock Fronts of Urban Decay and Criminal Behavior: How U,S. Cities Are Becoming Hollowed out"). Social ecologists have studied such neighborhoods and have linked the abject poverty to crime. ("Social Dlsorganlzatlon and Theorles of Crime and Dellnquency').

Thousands of studies have established a direct link between urban blight and crime. ("The Effects of Socioeconomic Disadvantage and Poverty Concentration on Homicide").

The government can help to reduce crime by providing more funds for social welfare programs. This has been a proven method to reduce crime, ("Reconsidering the Relationship Between Welfare Spending and Serious Crime"). Another aspect to this equation is how we address the so-called "War on Drugs." Addicts should be treated and not arrested. Being addicted to drugs is a public health issue and not a crime in of itself, Yet this is how the problem is currently being addressed in the criminal justice system. Drug courts are a good alternative to address public health problems linked 1o drug abuse.

Many crimes are drug related, "Drug courts provide an ideal setting to address these problems by linking the justice system with health services and drug treatment providers while easing the burden on the already overtaxed correctional system." ("Criminology: Theories, patterns and typologies").

The errors associated with the War on Drugs are endless, At the forefront are people of color being criminalized indiscriminately. Drug arrests make people eligible for housing, education grants, and welfare benefits which only exacerbate the problem. This pushes drug users further into a life of crime, Billions of tax dollars are wasted in this fight. Treatment is the solution. Group therapy, outpatient programs, residential care, counseling, detoxification, mental health care, and other alternative sources of treatment must be integrated to address drug addiction. ("DrugFacts: "Treatment Approaches for Drug Addlestone").

Non-violent offenders need to be rehabilitated instead of merely being warehoused in prison. Probation/Parole violators should be placed in community correctional centers instead of being sent back to prison. The 1994 Crime Bill to address violent crime has proved ineffective as well, There needs to be a varied approach to reducing violent crime. Making first-time violent offenders serve eighty-five percent of their sentences has not had a deterrent effect upon violent crime. ("Imprisonment and Crime: Can Both Be Reduced"). Even such measures as Three-strikes-And-Your out have not proven to have a deterrent effect upon crime. ("Proposition I and Crime Rates in California:The Case of the Disappearing Deterrent"). These violent offenders need rehabilitation also, Pell Grants need to be given back to prisoners as well. Statistics show that having a college education reduces a prisoner's recld vlsm rate to 65 percent.

The vast majority of prisoners will be released back out into society, Therefore it only maltes sense that more money be put into rehabilitating prisoners. If we fail to do this we will only continue to add to the problem of mass incarceration, Furthermore mass incarceration creates its own set of problems. It costs vast sums of money to incarcerate people. States now spend more of their budget on prisons than they do on education. The United States has over 2.5 million people in prison. Forty percent of these prisoners are over the age of 50, These older prisoners have cost the government and taxpayers bllllorts of dollars on healthcare due to a harsh prison environment that triggers health complications' A lot of these older prisoners no longer pose a threat to society because thov aged out of crimo. ("Crime and Urban Nature"). The only way to really put a dent into mass Incarcerailon is to allow some of our life sentenced prisoners to get a chance for parole one day if they prove themselves worthy of such, one out of ten prisoners is serving a sentence of life without parole or virtual life. ("Meaning of Life: Life Sentences in the United States"). Some of the terY- of thousands of prisoners serving this harsh sentence deserve a second chance. For those who no longer pose a threat, r. is only feasible for society to reevaluate their harsh sentences, If we do this it will really help us to reduce the prison population. Geriatric prisoners who have aged out of crime pose n0 threat to society and therefore we waste billions of dollars warehousing such humans in prison. In turn once we release the above prisoners they can add to the ta, base and help keep kids out of trouble as well as contribute to society in many ways with their life learned lessons irr prison, once we take these steps we can end the saga of mass incarceration, Ultimately, this will help us in all sectors of society.

Works Cited

McCaghy, Charles. "Deviant Behavior". (New York: MacMillan, 1976.) Print.

Sealock, Miriam. "Unraveling Bias In Arrest Decisions". Justice Quarterly 15 (1998): 427-457. Print.

Lewis, Oscar. "The Culture of Poverty". Scientific American 215 (1966) 19-25. Print.

Gunn, Jeanne. "The Effects of Poverty on Children". Future of Children 7 (1997): 34-39. Print.

Wallace, Rodrick. "Expanding Coupled Shock Fronts of Urban Decay and Criminal Behavior: How U.S. Cities Are Coming Hollowed Out". Journal of Quantitative Criminology 7 (1991) : 333-855. Print.

Bursik, Robert. "Social Disorganization and Theories of Crime and Delinquency". Criminology 26 (1998) : 519-522. Print.

Maume, Michael. "The Effects of Socioeconomic Disadvantage and Poverty Concentration on Homicicle". Rural Sociology 68 (2003) : 107-131. Print.

Worrall, John. "Reconsidering the Relationship Between Welfare Spending and Serious Crime". Justice Quarterly 22 (2005): 364-391. Print.

Siegel, J. Larry. "Criminology: Theories, Patterns and Typologies". (Boston: Cengage Learning, 2016): 536. Print.

National Institute on Drug Abuse. "DrugFacts: Treatment Approaches for Drug Addiction" (www.drugabuse.gov/publications/treatmentapproaches)

Durlauf, Steven. "Imprisonment and Crime: Can Both Be Reduced" Criminology and Public Policy. 10 (2011): 13-54. Print.

Webster, Cheryl. "Proposition B and Crime Rates in California: The Case of the Disappearing Deterrent". Criminology and Public Policy 5 (2006): 417-448. Print.

Wilson, James. "Crime and Human Nature". (New York: Simon and Schuster, 1985): 126-147. Print.

Mauer, Marc. "Meaning of Life: Life Sentences in America". (New York: Free Press 2018). Print.

Through the Darkness Find the Light Within You

At certain periods in our lives, things get denmark.
A future that once looked bright begins to look stark.
The light that used to illuminate before begins to fade.
A colorful picture of success distorts itself in shade.

All that was gained before is on the verge of being lost.
Some things can't be paid for in monetary cost.
When they count us out, we must get back up and fight again.
Every last that we take presents another chance to win.

Before dawn, we are overshadowed by the darkest hour.
Inside of yourself, you can make it through this using your will-power.
There is an inner light that shines through every dark moment.
Giving you vision which enlightens your path to overcome the opponent.

The enemy can even come from within.
A nagging doubt that you start to believe in. Why doubt when you have so much potential.

Denying yourself the victory although you pass every credential.

In the end, the light will always overpower the darkness.
See your way through adversity while evening out the odds of starkness.
A sharpened tooth bites through the dark
Let's give birth to success like a bird's beak cracking the egg to see light through the dark.

Unsung Heroes

There are a lot of everyday heroes that we don't hear about too often.
They do great works that we go uncelebrated on without a doubt.
I write this poem to give them the recognition that they are due.
Let's recognize the heroic deeds they do for me and you.

For the love of the people, they do this unpaid labor.
Helping thor fellow mankind without seeking recognition or favors.
Good Samaritans in every sense of the word.
These are the heroes of which we have never heard.

If you are a songwriter reading this, you should write a song for the unsung heroes.
Through your lyrics celebrate their actions so that the people can know.
Without your singing their praises, these heroes remain unknown.
So I implore you to write about them in your next song.

More super than a superhero because they are real.
Instinctively taking actions that heal.
Trying to keep up with their achievements will drive people berserk.

This is reality and not the mythical hero of a classic literary work.

There is a hero up and down every street.
These are ordinary people that we meet.

It's their extraordinary actions that makes their deeds glow.
Going beyond the call of duty, they are an unsung hero.

Sometimes You Have to Climb a Mountain to Get There

There are ____ when you will have to climb a mountain to reach your destination. This consists of hard work and won't be an easy form of recreating whether the place you are going is very far or a little ways away, the journey calls upon you to work hard by night as well as by the day.

Sharp rocks of life cut at your hand as you reach up for the ledge. You must not fall off the cliff when you get poked by a jagged edge. Don't get weak because you must constantly learn on this journey. Survival of the fittest evading getting pulled out on a gurney.

Remember this is your mountain and nobody else's to climb in order to set a record you don't have to be the greatest of all time. It is not always easy to get where we are trying to go in life. Climbing our own personal mountains is so full of strife.

However difficult it may be, we must learn to enjoy the journey while getting through our tribulations, we will learn so much wisdom to share. That's the true meaning of life when you are giving. Contributing something to this world is the real reason for living.

We have to move mountains to get to where we are trying to go. Moving against the terrain because there is no water where these dry rivers flow. There is just you and your will striving to make it to the valley. Put on your best gear so the forces of nature you can rally.

No matter how long it takes to get there, just keep climbing. Internalize the determination of each one of these verses I am rhyming. Look out over the horizon traveling down to the valley where your success is a skip and a hop.

Never Judge a Book by Its Cover

      We should never judge a book by its cover. On the inside, you never know what you might discover. When I use the word book, I am speaking in metaphor of all the people, places, and things that us human beings have a tendency to stereoty[e without even knowing its true essence. You can never know a thing when you are on the outside looking in. The only way that you can know for sure is by observing the contents within. We must learn discernment so that our preconceived notions will not cloud our judgment.

      It will definitely be a clear error in our past to decide not to read a book because of how it looks. A book cover serves as no more than a wrapping. In the marketing profession, they have a motto that says "packaging is everything." This statement cannot be taken out of context by the layman who needs to understand that just because the packaging is glossy does not mean that the product is good. We can't be sleeping on what is inside of a book because we failed to take a deeper look. A diamond does not lose its value because it was found inside of a piece of coal. A butterfly is no less beautiful just because it originated from a caterpillar. Yet if we were to judge those books by their cover we would assess their value to be far below their worth.

For insurance, if you had a shiny red corvette with no engine inside sitting next to a beat up Chevy Impala you would automatically be inclined to attribute a far greater worth to the red corvette. We have been programmed to think this way in a materialistic society that places value on things that are not worthy of the devotion that we give them. If we were to look at the contents of these things, we would see that the beat up Chevy Impala has a customized engine inside of it that is worth $50,000 with a customized interior that is worth $100,000. In total this car is valued at $200,000. On the other hand, the shiny red Corvette is only valued at $50,000. The beat up seemingly valueless Chevy Impala is worth four times more than the seemingly super expensive shiny red corvette. These are the wrong conclusions that we draw when we judge a book by its cover without knowing what is within it.

If a visitor from the free world would look around this room right now, all that he or she would see is a room full of men with gray uniforms. We would easily be stereotyped as criminals and lowlifes. Yet if that visitor was to listen to our conversation, he or she would see that we are much more than a common criminal. In fact, based on the content of our speeches, this free would citizen would conclude that we have a lot to offer society if given a chance to apply our various unique skill sets.

Looking at a book cover cannot tell you what the book is all about. A cover story is a story within itself. Look at the art. A picture is worth a thousand words. It would be foolish to judge a book without picking it up off the shelf. We can't scan through the pages and think we've got it all figured out. There could be one paragraph that we overlook that causes us to miss out on the moral of the story. Inside of that book could have been the answers to questions that you have for a long time. Therefore, failing to read a book because of how it looks would make a wrong decision. We must be deep enough to look within something before we form a judgment of its worth.

A book's cover does tell a story, but that's not the whole story. If a picture is worth a thousand words, then we must still miss out on the tens of thousands of other words inside of the book. All of our lives, people have been stereotyping us. We are books that have been judged by their covers. Since we know precisely how it is to be misunderstood, we should be the first not to judge a book by its cover.

It is the contents inside of the book that tells us what it is about. After we learn and study these contents, then and only then should we form a judgment about the book. In conclusion, I just want to remind each one of us that we should never judge a book by its cover.

A Mother's Burden   9-18-2020

A mother's duties are many
When it comes to worry. She has plenty.
She carries such a heavy load.
That's why it's so hard to get into relaxation mode.

Every decision that she makes affects her and her offspring.
She must think for herself as well as the children in everything
This means that she carries her own weight as well as theirs.
Upon herself is a lot of cares

Being a mother is the hardest job in the world.
It doesn't matter if the child is a boy or a girl.
A single mother has to take on the responsibility.
Even with the father's help, she still places on herself most of the liability.

During trying times, you can see the burden of the load and get heavy on her back
Still, she keeps moving ahead at a steady pace without giving any slack.
In spite of the difficulty, she carries her burden well.
Helping her children along the way so they won't fail.

A mother will sacrifice everything for her children.
She just wants to see them win.
Seeing her kids succeed in life is her duty.
Therefore, she picks up her load with pride as he carries a mother's burden.

A GARDEN in the Ghetto

Growing up in the inner city ghetto of St. Louis, Missouri did not allow our family to see many of nature's wonders. Our neighborhoods were full of vacant houses, broken down cars, drug dealers every which way you looked, gangbangers posted up and down the block, broken beer bottles loitering the sidewalks, yards with run down grass, streetlights that didn't work, etc. It was more like nature's curse rather than nature's gift.

There was, however, an exception. Ironically, it was right there in my own backyard. Yet, my mother had a small garden. When she first started the Thai garden, people looked at her like she was crazy. Her friends made comments such as: "girl what are you doing planting a garden in this dump." and Dee Dee do not waste your time because somebody will just steal your vegetables before you get them. "It will never work in this neighborhood, etc. Being the determined soul that she is, fortunately, my mother ignored the critics. She wanted her garden and she got it. Me being the curious child that I was. I watched her every step of the way.

She went into the backyard and tilled the hard worn soil. First, she would water it everyday, then she purchased a hoe and started turning over the soil. Once she did this for a while, she started planting the small seed that she got from the local hardware store. There wasa seeds for tomatoes, greens, lettuce, cucumbers, etc. I looked at the little seed packs and started shaking them and wondering how she could possibly grow something from these seeds in these bags. My mother is a proud lady so she went out into her garden everyday. She would put on her straw hat and be out in the blazing sun on her knees arranging the rows of the garden. She would spend hours out there while we were out front playing games. She would come in all sweaty to get a drink of water and then go back out there in her garden. People shook their heads at her but my mother did not care.

When it rained outside, she would just sit there staring out her window at her garden. After the rainfall, she would go back out there and adjust the soil. I never understood what she was doing. Nevertheless, in the few months everything that she planted blossomed. Right there in the ghetto, surrounded by drive-by shootings, drug deals, and extreme poverty, my mother's garden got really big in our backyard. It took over 80 percent of the backyard. When you stepped back there, all you could see was her garden, it was a beautiful sight. In the backdrop of an alley littered with trash and cracked concrete stood her picturesque garden. It had many colors. The greens were growing everything. She had yellow flowers back there, cucumbers, lettuce sprouting everywhere, and other stuff that I do not know the name of. It sure looked good though. And it tasted even better. She would have certain days where we ate entire meals made entirely from what she cooked in her garden.

Low and behold, those same neighbors who criticized her meager efforts started coming over asking her for some of the vegetables and other edibles that she was delicately growing. My mother never holds grudges and she was proud to share her fruits and vegetables with all of her neighbors. She would store a lot of what she grew in the house and give everything else away to her neighbor and her sisters. This became a sort of tradition for her. Despite how poor our family was, my mother would not allow poverty to define her. In our concrete city streets she created her own personal paradise. Despite all the negativity surrounding us, the kids could go into this garden and find some refuge of peace. It was our own little corner of the world. We did not do any of the gardening but just walking through it, we felt part of her garden. She had the rows all neatly spaced. She kept the dirt moist, etc.

I would sometimes see her out there in a lean chair, oblivious to the world, just sitting there drinking some tea. Staring chiling. Mama would have on some sandals and be so peaceful out there in her garden. She always created little small miracles. Rightnow to this day, 30 years later, I wonder how she did it? She always used to say that she was at peace in her garden. It was peaceful back there. She would sit in the garden with her own thoughts for hours. She would sit in the garden with her own thoughts for hours. She couldn't afford a vacation or go on a trip. Instead, she would get away from it all while sitting right there in her garden in the very troubled chaotic ghetto slum that we lived in. Like the rose that grew from the concrete, she defied the odds and grew a garden in a place where nature does not traditionally bloom. By refusing to allow the walls of hell to close in on her, my mother created her own paradise right there in the ghetto by way of her lovely garden.

When Adults can be Kids Again (While Having Fun)
7-26-2021

There is great joy when adults can enjoy themselves like kids again
True happiness is infectious and for everyone, it is a win-win
Life is so fulfilling when grown folks can just let go and be carefree
Acting up while having a good time, experiencing the world's beauty

When adults laugh from their gut, you see a mirror of their childhood
Long before life's burdens overwhelmed them when times were good
Being a kid is a time of wonder
Exploring life in fun while casting your cares asunder

Imagine as an adult re-capturing that blissful childhood joy
Feeling that youthful exuberance you felt as a girl or boy
With life so full of promise to explore
Sky's the limit and opportunity knocks behind every door

We can not allow the bad things in life to take away this childhood state of being
For a moment, visualize a child's way of seeing

Everything in life doesn't have to be complicated.
As kids, we made things simple even as we evaluated

Let's reflect on how it was back in the day
Better yet, we must recapture a piece of that today.
When we do, adults can be kids again while having fun
Experiencing an innocent joy that is second to none

A Piece of Peace 7-26-2021

Everyone just wants a little peace
A time of harmony when all of the madness cease
Most of us seek out peace however we can
That's the natural state of man

Mankind searches for peace in countless ways
In its essence is how we long to spend our days
Without peace a man or woman can't claim to be whole
This is why we search for peace in our soul

At times, we all just want a little peace and quiet
Moments of relaxation when our minds don't run riot
In the cocoon of our shell before we step out into the air
Just a moment of peace when we can put away our every care

With so much chaos going on, peace may seem hard to find
Nevertheless if we look hard enough we locate it right there in our mind
Peace doesn't have to be elusive
Its whereabouts are not exclusive

We search from without but ultimately peace comes from within
In all of our seeking this is where we must begin

As the quireness around us decreases
We just have to consume peace in bits and pieces

Internal Value v. External Value

Today I want to discuss the internal value of something versus the external value. The prefix of the word internal is (i.n), which means what is on the inside, The prefix to the external is (ex), which means on the outside, exit, or outer layer. In our modern materialistic society, we
often incorrectly give value to strings based on their external appearance.

Wisdom and discernment accumulated from life experiences will teach us that we must access value based on the internal. Let me give you an example or two of what I am talking about. If a man sees a woman who has a nice body and make up he is more likely to be attracted to her than the woman with big glasses who looks plain.

Making a judgment based on their externat value is his first mistake. See this man does not have children and his dream wife would be a good spiritual woman who raised his girls. The pretty woman with the nice body can not have kids and she has no real ambitions in life. On the other hand the nerdy looking woman is the CEO of her own jewelry company. She is actively looking for a husband to have kids with. But this man chose based on external appearance and missed out on his dream wife.

Here is a picture of a couple who look like they are very happy together. But internally their relationship is a disaster that has fallen apart. The picture Is not what it appears to be. In fact this couple is no longer together and in the middle of a divorce. They took this picture for sentimental purposes because they wanted to symbolically remember how happy they once were. This picture is only a goodwill memory.

Yet try looking at the external value of that picture we would reach the wrong conclusion. If we look at a new million dollar mansion sitting next to a century's old brownstone apartment building, we would automatically assume that the mansion is worth more. But the foundation of the mansion is not stable and it starts sinking in about a year. The brownstone will stand the test of time and last another century.

It is what is on the inside that carries the greatest value. Having a clean body does not mean that you have a pure soul. Just because something is new does not give it more value than the old. For instance, look at this picture of this new shiny red corvette versus this old beat up Chevy. The 2013 shiny Recl Corvette is worth $52,000. Now up under that we see an old Nova 1967 Chevy station wagon. At first appearance it seems like an old station wagon, But when you look inside and see what it is made of you realize its internal value verses the external value of the shiny red corvette" The old wagon has a tubed rear end worth $15,000, a new hippo engine worth $17,000, a box from worth $9,000, specialized titanium rims and tires worth $15,000, and a $5,000 transmission. Therefore, it is worth 3 times more than the shiny new red corvette.

This book here that I am holding looks way more fancy than this book. This book has a fancy design on it while this book has no design at all. But in this hand, I am holding the book which can change your life for the better if you follow its precepts. This book here is a science fiction book that only serves for entertainment purposes. Once you put it down you will forget about it. But the teachings of the book will stick with you.

The examples that I have given show us that we must stop placing so much emphasis on how something looks and focus on what it is made of. Let us learn this lesson now before we go through life choosing things based on the wrong external estimates. With that I hope that I have given you some valuable information in this speech. Thank you.

The Making of a Classic

Classic:

Everyday, someone is somewhere creating something. Whether they are creating music, a piece of art, writing a novel, book, or poen, designing a shoe, making a watch, or any other invention in life; for every second that passes by someone in the world is making something. Some of these things are what we call run-of-the-mill. Meaning that these articles serve some purpose but do not have a lasting impact upon history or inspire awe to the eye of the beholder. Every once in a while, though, we come across a thing, place, or person that has an impact upon us that nothing else has ever had before. In our frantic search to place this work of art in some plausible category, we are only left with one definition to truly sum it up, so we call it what it truly is: a classic.

When people behold a classic, their minds marvel at the genius which was blessed with such a wonderful gift to be able to create such a magnificent piece of art. How did they do it? Where did they get the elements to come up with such a concept? If you ask them you are likely to get such nonchalant answers as "I was just being creative," or "it just comes natural." But to the person not blessed with such gifts, such a feat to them can not be explained by nothing short of a miracle. Nature, the universe, and all of its elements has never inspired in them the creative juices to go outside of the norm. So a classic takes on all the more of a special morning in their life.

Now let's go to the origins of this? What is a classic?

Exactly what qualifies a work to be designated as a classic? (who said this statement? Look up John Johnson's autobiography in the chapter where he talks about the front streets) Someone once famously said that "you'll know classic when you see it." Meaning that the standard text compiled for this word fails to give its full shade of meaning. Additionally, some things in life just defy explanation. Classic is such a term. Although we attempt to put it in a category, it is uncategorizable. Classic; it is that creation that is over and beyond, something mystical in its own right. The making of a classic is usually a process born of humble origins. Periodically, though, even in the incomplete stages of the work, the creator senses that they have a classic on their hands. The challenge is that all the right ingredients must resonate all throughout the work. The term classic only attaches to works that are classic all the way through its entirety. Other terms "partly a classic" or "almost classic" fail to carry the weight necessary to tip the scales to arrive at the prestigious destination of classic. The work either meets the criteria or it doesn't.

In the modern age, you often hear artists say that they aspire to make their next piece of work a classic. They even undeservedly attach the word "classic" to their last piece of work which clearly did not meet those standards. It isn't the critics that classify a work as classic. Mainly it is the fans. Critics always find holes to poke in an artist's creation. If any little element is out of place, the critics' will highlight it and attempt to take away from the substance of the work. Ever so often though, an exceptional piece of work is created and even the critics have to accede to it being classic at the outset. History can be cruel and ironic, in that some classic works are not defined as a classic until decades or even centuries after their creation. For instance (). Some people, places or things were never considered a classic in their own time, yet were given the acclaim of a classic way after their prime.

When, where, and how is a classic created? The process of making a classic can not be limited to a time capsule or consumed by boundaries. Such artificial barriers cannot contain the genius that is responsible for making classics. Throughout history classics have been created in the most oppressive and repressive countries. Numerous classics have often emerged from a prison cell. Time and place may take on a historical backdrop in classic works, but even when a classic is describing a time and place, this in itself can never limit the genius and universal elements that went into the making of that classic. The making of a classic is a process that happens when the artist goes into a deeper place inside of themselves and uses that raw, rare genius that is bigger than themselves. The elements of the universe magically assemble through this person's mind and soul and they share it with the world. The process sometimes seems divine. That's how difficult it is to explain at times.

The making of a classic can be likened to the process of chemistry. It's like going into the lab with these potent substances and mixing it up thereby manufacturing (or some other word) a special concoction. Although some of the elements came from the maker of the classic, the end result of the art is bigger than them. It becomes a relic of history for everybody to share. It has its own special meaning to everyone who encounters such a classic. Such classics take on such a rarity that when the creator of the classic prepares for an exhibit or a live performance they don't go through what you;ll call a routine rehearsal because even a rehearsal can't prepare them for what actually happens when that live element is taking place. It isn't like an ordinary performance because when you do something classic it is you and the evidence sharing a deeper part of your souls with each other. In the process of you giving them the art and then receiving it, each person is taken to a deeper place than where they are actually at. It is difficult to explain in words, but when it happens everyone there knows that it was classic.

Now often when we think of classical literature, we think of something from times gone by (decades or centuries ago). A substantial body of classical literature is created in those contemporary times as well. When people think of true rare classical music they often reach back into the archives of history and attach such music to a few prestigious musicians. The same can be said of art and the other classic articles. Need we again explain what classic is? Okay, thus we have talked about classic creations, but what makes a person a landmark to the point where we defined him or her as classic.

A classic person is one of a kind. It \'s a magical mysterious personality. A historical figure, not only those who have been recorded by history but those who are historical in their own right. It's in how they move, how they walk, how they talk. Everything about them is classic. Nevertheless, the reader must know that just because something or someone is classic, that does not necessarily translate into success for that person or thing. Classic can even be in the making of. Most people who create classics in one area have failed in so many other areas. It was their dogged determination to succeed that led to their making a classic. In fact, it was that raw hunger and bitter thirst for success that allowed them to pull something out of themselves that is deeper than them that translated into this classical gem. They failed so many times that they were determined to make it big at something. So many mistakes were made along the way. Such failures were used as a motivation for success and a stepping stone to reach the heights. When they failed hard, they tried even harder to succeed.

Even in their failures a whisper in their souls tells them that they are capable of achieving so much. Despite numerous losses and countless personal tragedies they are determined to make something out of nothing. So they turn to art and create the impossible. Speaking of which, some of the greatest works in history were created out of a mode of depression. Sometimes, in their failures these artists and authors have lost everything and nothing sustains them but their own personal dreams. The critics scoff at them, the taunters doubted them, and the haters damned their artistry. Despite all this, they kept dreaming. In the meantime, they were just gathering all the key elements, raw materials, and forces of nature to create a masterpiece. Sometimes these were just a once in a lifetime masterpiece and at other times, the classics came in abundance. One has to admire how a person turned tragedy into triumph, how a person comes back from the verge of defeat, and succeeds against the odds. History is full of examples of such legends. The decks were stacked against them yet they prevailed despite going against the grain. Somehow they made something out of nothing. They created a miracle right before our eyes while we are still trying to figure out how they did it. And in their story and legend is what I call the making of a classic.

A place that is classic can be described in the experience of the visitors to that place. Sometimes a place is so classic that this can be seen from the outside looking in or recorded through history in text. Such places definitely inspire awe. First we wonder how such a place was built? Who came up with such a grand architectural plan? Some of these places are man-made while the others have been created by the forces of nature. These abodes are so mesmerizing. No form of imitation can capture their originality. These places give you a special experience within themselves. Their essence is mystique. Without words, without oral tradition, and without hieroglyphics these classic places tell you their own story in a way that no man can. When you enter these places you somehow feel an unexplainable connection with its past. It is hard to separate your own existence from the existence of this place, because somehow you feel so connected to the place. Such A feeling is what is known as a classic experience.

Within the known and unknown traditions about the origins of these places is the stuff of legend. There are extraordinary stories told about the making of these places. The stories are unique in themselves. Even so, the appeal of these places takes on an identity independent of their origins. Decades and even centuries of intense study still cannot explain some things about such places. How they were made defy human explanation, although we've since learned how some of them were made. Thus these places are what classic is within itself; simply unexplainable because definition is too simple to explain it.

We must not forget that there are many forces at work during the making of a classic. Despite popular legend and myth, many times the making of a classic is surrounded by hostility, heartbreak, depression, and in some cases outright sabotage. Such factors definitely can come into play when a classic is created through collaboration. In these situations the making of the classic has its own unique story to tell which makes the art even more outstanding considering the underlying circumstances. The collaboration process is special in itself because you have the minds of two or more people creating something. In turn, there is the cohesion or conflict of personality clash; the different directions that each contributor wants to take the art in and the different visions that each artist has for the work. Writers even go through this in the editorial process. So when you factor all these diverse elements into play and the work turns out to be a classic, such dynamic art, rightfully deserves a palace in history.

Classics came from many places, emotions, and things. Classics come from a place of pain and sometimes they come from the greatest joy. Some people are genius enough to create a classic while simply having fun. The creator of the classic is sometimes surprised at the results. Consumers purchase so many things that they know a classic when they come across one. It is that special thing that stands the test of time. That classic thing is when someone does something no one else has ever done or does it in a way that has never been done before leaves you in awe. It is simply amazing. Define it though we may try, classic is in the eye, ear, and feel of the beholder.

The Responsibility of Being a Parent

Being a parent is the hardest job in the world. This is because you are responsible for another person's life. YOU are the infant's first teacher. Whatever the child grows up to be will be traced back to your efforts in raising the child. The nurturing of a child begins in the womb even before birth. Medical tests have proven that while it is in the mother's womb the child hears the voices in its environment. The mother must get the proper prenatal care in order to deliver a healthy fetus.

The mother has much more responsibility than the father. Her responsibilities begin once she finds out that she is carrying an embryo in her womb. Her entire life changes forever from the day forward. She becomes not responsible for her own life but she also becomes responsible for the life inside of her womb. Every decision that she makes will affect the child's future. Seh becomes more conscious of how she moves around so that she may protect the child in her womb. She eats for two people now instead of eating for one.

With today's modern medical advancements, the mother is required to get certain vaccination shots even before the infant is born. Once the baby is born, the parents are responsible for getting the baby certain vaccinations for such diseases as polio, measles, smallpox flu viruses, etc.

When a child comes out of the womb, the parents hold the power of life and death for the child. This is the most important responsibility that a person can have in life. Whatever the child grows up and becomes will be a reflection on the parents. This is why a parent must give their best in nurturing their child. A newborn baby is a gift to the parents but the child also casts a lot of responsibility upon the parent.

The parent's individuality takes a backseat to their new role as primary caregiver. They must put the child's best interest before their own interest. Every decision that they make affects the child's life. This means that a parent must think for themselves as well as their child.

Although I'm not a parent, I have read so many books on parenting that I have lost count. Believe me, I have done my research on this subject. Furthermore, I have witnessed numerous parents raise children in my own household, neighborhood, and through parents I have met over the years. Even though parenthood carries a lot of responsibility, we humans are equipped with the needed abilities to raise children.

Being a parent is not just a burden but it comes with great joy. There is no greater joy than raising a child. Being a parent is priceless. It enables you to form a relationship with another human like no other relationship you have ever known. You are connected to the child through DNA, blood and ancestral ties.

A parent is so proud when their child accomplishes a goal. The parent knows that their hard work in raising the child was not in vain. Furthermore, the parent understands that they are partially responsible for the child's success. Therefore, they both share in the victory of accomplishment.

There are so many rewards to being a parent. I look forward to one day becoming a parent. I know that the responsibility will not be easy but it is well worth the effort. We have many experiences in this short life but none of them can equal the opportunity to serve in the capacity of handling the responsibilities of being a parent.

All My Life

Three-Fourths of my entire life have been spent inside of a prison cell. Since the age of 16 years, I have been incarcerated. I am 41 years old now. More than a quarter of a century accounts for 75% of my life confined in jail. Forever fighting off the stigma of being institutionalized, I hold on clearly to my memories of the streets. Besides all of the knowledge that I've learned here as well as the things that I've accomplished I have been in prison for what feels like "All My life."

The quick 16 years that I spent in the free world doesn't nearly compare to the long hard slow 25 years of suffering that I've spent in prison. Yet I must not lose sight of my victims and the people I've harmed. I am not innocent. This is no pity party my story represents too much redemption for that). I celebrate the good along with the bad. I say this to point out the fact that I came to prison as a child and I've been here for nearly "All My Life."

I dislike prison. I dream of leaving here everyday. For 25 years, this is all that I've known. In a few more years, I will have been locked up for twice as long as I was in the free world. That time is creeping up fast. My harsh sentence for 241 years has been universally condemned but due to justice being denied I am slowly rotting away inside of a prison cell for "All My Life" (according to the State of Missouri).

Prison hurts. It hurts your body, it hurts your bones, hell, it even hurts your soul. I see so many men become bitter here. This place eats them alive. So much misery stews inside of them that nothing comes out of their mouth but hate. They hate the world, they even hate themselves. So what do they have to lose? A man in here will stab you for jumping the line in front

The Art of GARDENING

The gardener is an artist, a creator, and an architect." A gardener is an artist because they create their garden in slow motion like a painter trying to get the colors. A sculptor tries to chisel his work exquisitely. A gardener does the same thing with their garden. The serenity in the garden sings to their soul.

Like any other form of art, gardening has to be mastered. You learn it as you are being taught. However, the garden teaches you, it becomes the teacher. It will reprimand you like a stubborn pupil. If your mind poses a question to the garden, it will not give you a direct answer, rather it will challenge you to discover every dimension will be of a miraculous nature. What is even more is how a garden amazes its creator.

When a garden is complete, its creator marvels at its beauty. Looking at it from afar, the gardener wonders how they themselves created something so wonderful.

All of the marvelous plants of varying colors sprouting towards the sky, pointed towards the sun they seem to want to take flight at any minute. Gardens are full of many layers, but each plant has its own unique story to tell. As you sit in the garden listening quietly to your own thoughts. You also hear the story of the garden being whispered to you in a small voice. Gardens are so full of life that you feel so alive in the midst.

At times, the toil of laboring in a garden can be intense. Gardening is hard work, yet it is a worthy effort. Therefore, people look forward to this work. For the dedicated gardener it becomes a sort of love affair.

Gardening is a work of art, and art takes hard work. When you see a breathtaking painting you know that someone put countless hours of work in its creation. A garden requires even more hours of labor. You have to work with the raw elements of nature. Insects can become either the garden's enemy or its friend. As the steward of the garden you try to balance it all out.

So many elements of nature give the garden life, yet many other elements of nature attempt to suffocate the garden. Chief among these elements is the weeds. Weeding must be painstakingly done by hand. One has to be diligent while constantly pulling weeds making sure that they do not attempt to choke the life out of the plants you are growing. Look at the painted picture and see all of its layers. It took a lot of master strokes from the painter's hand to get it right. As equally beautiful, the sight of an exquisite garden should stop you in your tracks. Each row is hard to be nurtured, watered, and carefully spaced apart at intervals. Seeds had to be carefully planted, etc. The garden has to get the right amount of light as well as sunshine. So many countless dynamics go into a garden's formation.

Like any other work of art, gardening is its own architecture. It is handcrafted. Designed from scratch, its blueprint is constructed on a parcel of earth. Its construction requires the gardener to take on many roles. Though uneducated in these various fields the gardener puts on the hat of an engineer, an ecologist, a botanist, a poet (a garden is poetic as it sings its own verses), a farmer, a mathematician, a biologist, etc. The science that the gardener learns from each of these disciplines allows them to make their garden into a work of art. A gardening school could never really teach you every facet of the art of gardening. A lot of it is learned through trial and error. Most of what you ultimately discover will be self taught. After you make your mistakes and learn along the way you will become a master of your garden. Once it is complete, it will take your breath away, not only from the hard work but ultimately because of its beauty and tranquility. You will marvel at your garden's beauty. Saying to yourself how beautiful it is, you will know at that moment that you have finally discovered the art of gardening.

You will Become Someone's Mother One Day

In the eyes of a child, their mother is their first teacher. She is everything to them. We often hold our mothers to the highest standard. Nevertheless, our mothers were once young and they have a past. They are only humans and they make mistakes too. So I just wanted to take a little time here to remind young women of their high position in the world. When you are in your teenage years, you are not considering the long-term consequences of your decisions. However, you must remind yourself that you will become someone's mother one day.

I respect my mother to the fullest but I still hurt in my soul when I think about her flaws and mistakes. She has been deceased over twenty years but I still feel pain when I recall her worst errors in life. That is how precious my mother is to me. This is how the vast majority of people feel about their mother. We just hold them to such a high standard. Yet they cannot imagine this as the young teenagers and young women living their lives. As young teenagers, they never could envision that we would one day critique their mistakes when we become teenagers. Young people don't think that far ahead. But young women I want you to really think about this. Really contemplate what I have written here.

As our mothers you mean so much to us. We do not hold you under a microscope but your actions are very big to us. We trip off of the things that our mothers did when she was young. We scrutinize her actions as a young woman from a place of pain. Her mistakes do not make her fall from grace in our eyes but her mistakes hurt us inside. It is a raw pain. She must understand that she is our mother. The woman that she became does not reflect the young woman of errors that she once was.

So young women while you are living your day-to-day life partying, having fun, or whatever else you may be doing, I want you to slow down for a moment and realize that you will be a mother one day. To your kids, you are everything to them. Even before they were born, you were their mother. Young women, please reflect upon your actions because your children will one day reflect on your actions. Think about what you are doing and how it will look in your children's eyes. Your mistakes pain your children's heart because you mean so much to them. So in your everyday doings, please remember that you will be someone's mother one day.

Vision: Coming into Focus

Envision in your mind's eye what you want to do and eventually the full plan will come to you. At first, it will come to you in bits and pieces. In time, it will congeal into a full blown blueprint. Visions originate from the most unusual sources. If we are not paying attention we will not grasp the vision when it presents itself to us. A wise man once said that opportunity presents itself dressed up as a problem. We just have to figure out a creative way to solve the problem. In order to do this our vision must come into focus.

The dictionary defines vision as: (1) something seen otherwise by ordinary sight (2) vivid picture created by the imagination; (3) the act or power of imagination; (4) unusual wisdom in foreseeing what is going to happen; (5) to conceive; (6) to form a mental picture of; (7) visualize. When people see something other than by ordinary sight, it seems to come to them out of nowhere. A light goes on in their head and they experience what we call an aha moment.

Visions must be acted on or they fade away. They are a powerful motivator for action. They show us the way. If we follow this path, we can fulfill our life's purpose. I am not speaking about some fly-by-night vision. I am talking about an all enduring soul deep vision. The kind that stirs a deep desire inside of you that you can't ignore even if you wanted to. It plants a seed inside of you that just keeps on germinating. Once it grows it becomes the most powerful desire in your life; overpowering all lesser desires. This vision becomes all consuming and demands your attention.

Once this vision comes into focus, it will give you the tools needed to carry out the job. No matter how difficult the task at hand may be, this vision will push you uphill until you reach the summit. Once there, you will be able to look out upon the valley of success visualizing your vision coming full circle. Imagination will give you the pieces to fill the puzzle. This vision is yours; thereby it's only something that you can do. It calls upon you to act upon it. Act on it now. The urgency of the vision will drive you forward. Onward push as you tackle the obstacles in front of you. Now the impossible seems possible.

All of the little steps that you took turn into one big step. You climb your personal mountain and move on to other peaks. The process repeats itself with other visions. Some goals will be much harder to achieve than others. Your past accomplishments will give you an unusual wisdom in foreseeing an uncharted path laid out before you. With each milestone reached, you will do what others before you thought couldn't be done. A pioneer in your own lane as your vision comes into focus.

Forged from Pain (Ode to Aretha Franklin) 2-12-2021

There is more to her story than fortune and fame
Her sucess was hard and foged from pain
Don't be blinded by all the glitter
In order to shine she had to throw away tons of litter

Only if you knew all of the pain she endured
Carrying a burden heavy enough to break a floorboard
Her genius was channeling this pain into her craft
Packing it for the masses so they could withstand life's wrath

She had her first child when she was young
Making your heart do a double take
When you hear the wisdom that flows from her tongue
When you was down what she said always made you feel uplifted
Amazed at her talent and how she was so gifted

Like a bridge over troubled water , she helped us get through
Something in her soul rings so true.
Out of the bottomless pit of poverty she rose to great heights.
Never forgetting when she was hungry and tired all those nights.

Pain takes a stake in our lives and gives us a challenge of what to do with it
She mastered this foe and conquered with her wit
Nowadays all that she epitomizes, is symbolized when we scream say her name
Little do people know that the accomplishments of her legacy were forged from pain

Nothing Like

There is nothing like a woman and her beauty
To love and protect them is every man's duty
Mother, daughter, sister, and auntie
Grandma is the matriarch of the family

Women are so strong
The miracle without which we couldn't get along
Look at the strength and care on her face
Lovely with natural grace

Nothing like a woman because without her, we can't survive
Without my mother's sacrifice, I wouldn't be alive
God thank you for giving us this wonderful creation
To every woman I send out this dedication

Bodies so beautiful when they walk
Sweet wounds flow from their mouths when they talk
Oh how I love a woman's personality
No matter if they are humble, diva-like, or sassy

One of a kind each one of them is original
Unique offering the world so much as an individual
I salute women and put them on a pedestal
There's nothing like a woman and they are so cool

Domestic Household Politics 11-15

No politics is more fragile than those of the common household
Each party is finally grounded in their platform and seldom willing to compromise or fold
It's difficult to choose sides when both persons have a valid position
Who do you vote for when you want to better everyone's condition?

The pros and cons have to be weighed
Otherwise the most articulate speaker will have your opinion swayed
Chores, bathroom privileges, meals, entertainment, allowances, and curfews are all on the agenda
Cheapskates taking on the guise of moderates reigning in liberals who don't budge like a big splenda

Siblings play political games while parents make the ultimate political play
Presidential they can veto bills if things don't go their way
At home, campaigns are often launched about almost any and everything
Who wins is the party that has the most benefits to bring

Briberty, calling in favors, and backroom deals is politics that go on in the house
Underhand tactics are used such as causing a rift between a husband and his spouse
Politicas can be dirty when they are played unfair
So when you throw your hat into the ring, beware

Elections, take place often as positions are vacated, abandoned, or often neglected
New offices must be fulfilled as an entire fresh political view is reflected
Vote from your conscience while avoiding being fool by the complex tricks
Each one of us grew up under the dominion our family's domestic household politics

The Water of Woman's Tears   11-13-21

Feel the water of a woman's tears
They carry the weight of emotions held back for years
Coming from a level that is soul deep
Yeah their pain does run that steep

We all know that a woman cries when she gives birth
Yet she also cries when she is happy and mirth
Emotional is the form in which she was made
Her feelings are often raw and fully loaded

A woman is created like no other being
She has empathetic eyes with a sensitive way of seeing
So their world for her is a place to love, take care, and cherish
Nothing beautiful in the universe does she wish to perish

When it is real pain that makes a woman cry
You want to help heal her instead of just asking why
What is it that caused her to cry in the first place
Is it not a pretty sight to see her with those tears on her face?

Her tears carry the power to clean the world of its dirt

Purified in her maternal instincts God knows how much she hurts
Pain from what she has been through and what she sees in the world everyday
She cries because she wishes things didn't have to be this way

The chemicals that come from the water of her tears consist of so many elements
Pain mixed with disappointment at the many tragedies and accident
Again she cries this way because the pain accumulated over several years
This is why there is no water deeper than a woman's tears

What you Go Through Helps You Get Through
1-14-21

There was a time or two when you thought you couldn't make it
Yet somehow through sheer survival, you overcame using your wit
They wrote you off and counter you out
Then thorough your hard work, you proved what determination is about

You found the strength to endure just when you thought you couldn't hold on any longer
Giving truth to the old saying "whatever doesn't kill you makes you stronger"
If it weren't for your past struggles, you wouldn't be the person you are today
This is reality and not just something to sound cliche

Everything you've gone through serves to point you towards your future destination
Follow the roadmap laid out in front of you with no hesitation
You already know what you need to do to achieve your life goal
Completing this mission is the only thing that will make you feel whole

Throughout your lifetime, you will wear many a hat

Only in hindsight will you learn why you went through this or that
Looking back should teach you how to go forward in a better way
Meanwhile you must learn to make the best of today.

Find something good in what everyone else sees as bad
Be an innovator while creating beautiful art in something that was once only regular plains
Bounce back from your troubles without letting your mistakes define you
Remember what you go through helps you get through

Dreams Die if We Let Them Sleep

They say that biggest graveyard on earth is full of dead men's dreams
Because people don't fulfill their life's purpose, it is bursting at the seems
Dreams only stay alive when we keep them woke
We must take action fulfilling the voice that our vision spoke

You have to be determined to carry your dreams out
Believe in the impossible while letting the doubters doubt
Start from scratch with an idea and build it into enterprise
Ignore the critics when they criticize

Things aren't always what they seem
Nothing comes to a sleeper but a dream
Two above sayings that we have all heard before
They only have meaning when you feel them at your core

Nobody can make your dreams come true but you
This means that you have a lot of work to do
You must start now right where you stand
Right before your eyes opportunities are all over the land

Work with tools you have at your disposal to get started
This hard labor is not for the weak or faint-hearted
Just to keep toileting the soil and eventually you'll reap what you sow
Taking small steps at first will allow your achievements to grow

We all deserve to take a rest or a quick name
In between the spaces, we must use success t fill in the gap
Remember from what we sow is what we reap
Our dreams will die if we let them sleep

Vision: Coming Into Focus
12-9-2021

Envision in your mind's eye what you want to do and eventually the full plan will come to you. At first, it will come to you in bits and pieces. In time, it will congeal into a full blown blueprint. Visions originate from the most unusual sources. If we are not paying attention, we will not grasp the vision when it presents itself to us. A wise man once said that opportunity presents itself dressed up as a problem. We just then have to figure out a creative way to solve the problem. In order to do this our vision must come into focus.

The dictionary defines vision as: (1) something seen otherwise then by ordinary sight; (2) vivid picture created by the imagination; (3) the act or power of imitation; (4) unusual wisdom in foreseeing what is going to happen; (5) to conceive; (6) to form a mental of; (7) visualize. When people see something other than by ordinary sight it seems to come to them out of nowhere. A light goes off into their head and they experience what we call an aha moment.

Visuals must be acted on or they fade away. They are a powerful motivator for action. They show us the way. If we follow this path, we can fulfill our life's purpose. I am not speaking about some fly-by-night vision. I am talking about an all enduring soul deep vision. The kind that stirs a deep desire inside of you that you can't ignore even if you wanted to. It plants a seed inside of you that just keeps germinating. Once it grows, it becomes the most powerful desire in your life; overpowering all lesser desires. This vision becomes all consuming and demands your attention.

Once this vision comes into focus. It will give you the tools needed to carry out the job. No matter how difficult the task at hand may be, this vision will push you uphill until you reach the summit. Once there, you will be able to look out upon the valley of success, visualizing your vision coming full circle. Imagination will give you the pieces to fill the puzzle. This vision is yours; thereby it's only something that you can do. It calls upon you to get upon it. Act on it now. The urgency of the vision will drive you forward. Onward push as you tackle the obstacles in front of you. Now the impossible seems possible.

All of the little steps that you took turn into one big step. You climb your personal mountain and move on to other peaks. The process repeats itself with other visions. Some goals will be much harder to achieve than others. Your past accomplishments will give you an unusual wisdom in foreseeing an uncharted path laid out before you. With each milestone reached, you will do what others before you thought couldn't be done. A pioneer in your own lane as your vision comes into focus.

Through the Darkness Find the Light Within You 9-18-2020

At certain periods in our lives things can get dark
A future that once looked bright begins to look stark
The light that use to illuminate before begins to fade
A colorful picture of success distorts itself in shade

All that was gained before is on the verge of being lost
Some things can't be paid for in monetary cost
When they count us out, we must get back up and fight again
Every lost that we take presents another chance to win

Before the dawn we are overshadowed by the darkest hour
Inside of yourself you can make it through this using your will-power
There is an inner light that shines through every dark moment
Giving you vision which enlightens your path to overcome the opponent

The enemy can even come from within
A nagging doubt that you start to believe in
Why doubt when you have so much potential

Denying yourself the the victory although you possess every credential

In the end the light will always overpower the darkness
See your way through adversity while evening out the odds of starkness
A sharpened tooth bites through the bark
Let's give birth to success like a bird's beak cracking the egg to see light through the dark

Bobby

www.ingramcontent.com/pod-product-compliance
Lightning Source LLC
Chambersburg PA
CBHW080348170426
43194CB00014B/2720